## Our Community Helpers

# Veterinarians Help

by Dee Ready

Consulting editor: Gail Saunders-Smith, PhD

CAPSTONE PRESS
a capstone imprint

Pebble Books are published by Capstone Press,
1710 Roe Crest Drive, North Mankato, Minnesota 56003
www.capstonepub.com

**Library of Congress Cataloging-in-Publication Data**
Cataloging-in-Publication information is on file with the Library of Congress.
ISBN: 978-1-62065-083-7 (library binding)
ISBN: 978-1-62065-851-2 (paperback)
ISBN: 978-1-4765-1721-6 (ebook PDF)

## Note to Parents and Teachers

The Our Community Helpers set supports national social studies
standards for how groups and institutions work to meet individual
needs. This book describes and illustrates veterinarians. The images
support early readers in understanding the text. The repetition of
words and phrases helps early readers learn new words. This book
also introduces early readers to subject-specific vocabulary words,
which are defined in the Glossary section. Early readers may need
assistance to read some words and to use the Table of Contents,
Glossary, Read More, Internet Sites, and Index sections of the book.

Printed in the United States of America in Stevens Point, Wisconsin.
092012    006937WZS13

# Table of Contents

# What Is a Veterinarian?

Veterinarians, or vets, are doctors who care for animals. Vets help sick animals. They also help healthy animals stay that way.

Different kinds of veterinarians care for different animals. Nearly half of vets treat cats, dogs, and other pets. They work at animal hospitals.

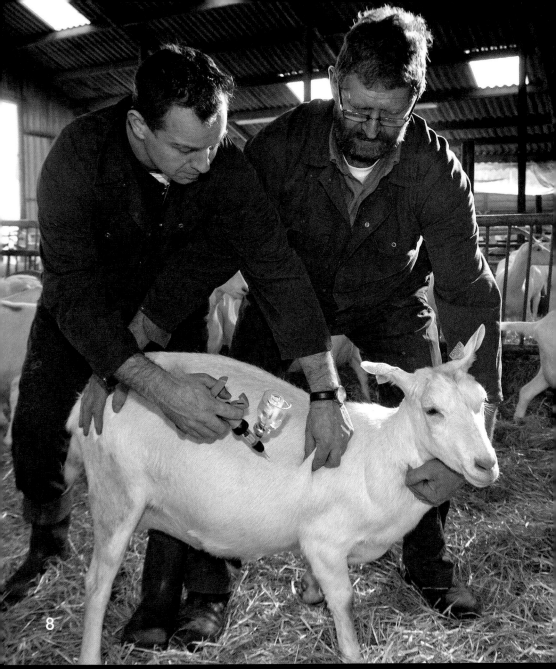

Other vets treat farm animals or horses. Farm animal vets visit the animals on farms.

Zoo vets work at zoos.
They treat the wild animals
kept in zoos.

## What Vets Do

Veterinarians try to make sick animals better. They set broken bones. They give medicine. Sometimes they operate to help sick animals.

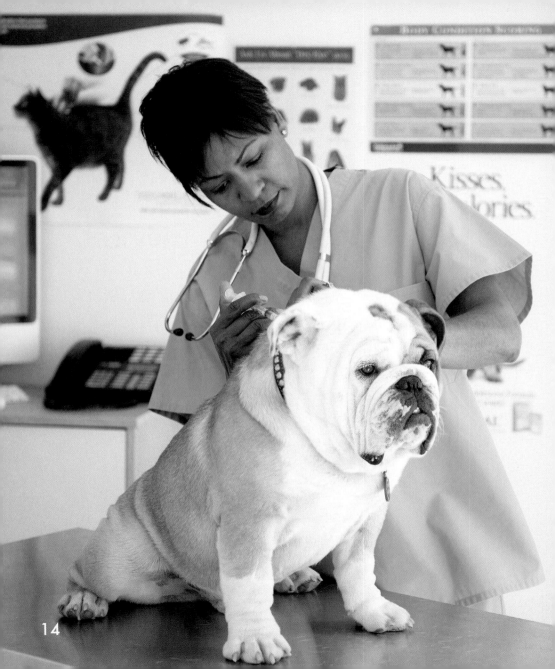

Veterinarians also give checkups to healthy animals. They give animals vaccinations to keep them healthy.

# Clothes and Tools

Veterinarians at hospitals wear lab coats and scrubs. Veterinarians at zoos and farms wear coveralls to keep their clothes clean.

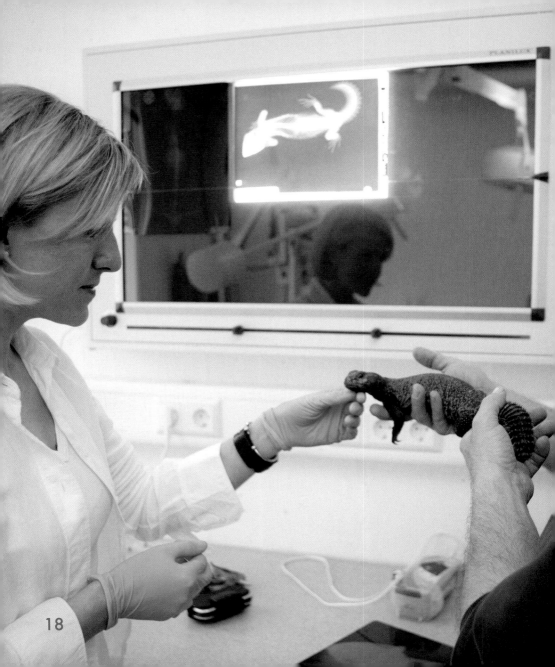

Veterinarians use the same kinds of tools as doctors. They use stethoscopes to hear heartbeats. They use x-rays to see inside sick or hurt animals.

# Veterinarians Help

Vets help wild animals, farm animals, and pets. They even help people by showing them how to care for their animals.

# Glossary

**healthy**—fit and well, not sick

**hospital**—a building where doctors and others work to help sick or hurt people or animals

**medicine**—a substance used to help sick people or animals get better

**operate**—to give medical treatment where the body is cut open

**scrubs**—a loose, lightweight uniform worn by workers in clinics and hospitals

**stethoscope**—a tool used to listen to the heart and lungs

**vaccination**—a shot of medicine that protects from a disease

**x-ray**—a picture taken of the inside of the body that can show if something is wrong

# Read More

**Ames, Michelle**. *Veterinarians in Our Community.* On the Job. New York: PowerKids Press, 2010.

**Lyons, Shelly**. *If I Were a Veterinarian.* Dream Big! Mankato, Minn.: Picture Window Books, 2011.

**Macken, JoAnn Early**. *Veterinarians.* People in My Community. New York: Gareth Stevens Pub., 2011.

# Internet Sites

FactHound offers a safe, fun way to find Internet sites related to this book. All of the sites on FactHound have been researched by our staff.

Here's all you do:

Visit *www.facthound.com*

Type in this code: 9781620650837

Super-cool stuff!

Check out projects, games and lots more at
**www.capstonekids.com**

# Index

**Word Count: 174**
**Grade: 1**
**Early-Intervention Level: 19**

**Editorial Credits**
Gillia Olson, editor; Gene Bentdahl, designer; Eric Manske, production specialist

**Photo Credits**
Alamy: Bill Bachman, 16, Chico Sanchez, 12, Olaf Doering, 18; Capstone Studio: Karon Dubke, 4, 6, 20; Getty Images: AFP/Sergei Supinsky, 10, The Image Bank/ LWA, 14; Newscom: EPA/Ed Oudenaarden, 8; SuperStock Inc.: Blend Images, cover